ORCHID HEART ELEGIES

THE HUGH MACLENNAN POETRY SERIES

Editors: Allan Hepburn and Carolyn Smart

Orchid Heart Elegies

ZOË LANDALE

McGill-Queen's University Press

Montreal & Kingston • London • Chicago

ISBN 978-0-2280-1439-3 (paper)
ISBN 978-0-2280-1544-4 (ePDF)
ISBN 978-0-2280-1545-1 (ePUB)

Legal deposit fourth quarter 2022
Bibliothèque nationale du Québec

Printed in Canada on acid-free paper that is 100% ancient forest free
(100% post-consumer recycled), processed chlorine free

Funded by the Government of Canada   Financé par le gouvernement du Canada | Canada   Canada Council for the Arts   Conseil des arts du Canada

We acknowledge the support of the Canada Council for the Arts.

Nous remercions le Conseil des arts du Canada de son soutien.

Library and Archives Canada Cataloguing in Publication

Title: Orchid heart elegies / Zoë Landale.

Names: Landale, Zoë, 1952– author.

Series: Hugh MacLennan poetry series.

Description: Series statement: The Hugh MacLennan poetry series

Identifiers: Canadiana (print) 20220283761 | Canadiana (ebook)
20220283788 | ISBN 9780228014393 (softcover) |
ISBN 9780228015444 (PDF) | ISBN 9780228015451 (ePUB)

Classification: LCC PS8573.A5315 O73 2022 |
DDC C811/.54—dc23

This book was typeset by Marquis Interscript in 9.5/13 Sabon.

CONTENTS

ORCHID HEART ELEGIES

Who among the quicksilver dead can reach through
   to comfort
when you weep? Even if one held out its arms,
you would drift through that much-wanted embrace
the way mist skirls through dark forest or fir pollen puffs
copper grains on the breeze. For death balances
on the cusp between the longèd-for and panic we can only
just endure. We worship this silence because it
   calmly refuses
to annihilate us. Each of our dead is sealed, a cipher
there's no reading in this lifetime.
So you endure this longing, its hook hard-set.
Who will help you?
Mystery's gold meaning which organizes us all
into lines of light? Even the animals understand
the insecurity of our perch; we are high-wire acrobats
about to tumble from the surface of the planet. Everything
we perceive is merely a guess. In the end,
all that's left is the yew tree you watch every day
from your window, silhouette black against the sky.
And our friend repetition, loyal as a dog;
the tidying of cluttered rooms,
the spun-silk habits of keeping a life clean.
Between the covers of waking and not,

a great windy terror scours your heart raw.
You reach out, sigh, remembering. Who can stay behind
when death summons? You are not immune.
From two, one is left.
Don't you get it? Open your arms, invite emptiness;
maybe your ghosts will feel the *whuff* of displaced air
and blow you a kiss.

It's true April had you on its short-list. White stars
of wild cherries to be admired. White boils of current
along the old village site, flood-tide rising
in green braids of current saying, *See?* And you did see
events, the why of betrayals from years ago
as you walked the beach, listened to the *cronk* of
    Canada geese
swimming ten feet away, suffering you balefully.
Weren't you always just about to pay
attention, each round minute rolling away? Sins
    of omission.
Will you blink now, zip sideways into the moving water
of your own life and go straight home
to a glass of wine? (There's no denying your cupboards
    are packed
with memories in hand-sewn cotton bags with ties.
The tenderness those ties provoke!)
If you breathe just so, the intensity slacks off.

You never understood before what a valiant act
being alive really is. Faces from the past peer
over your shoulder, particular about wanting to
    be noticed:
a boy with straw-coloured hair;
a woman who smells of face powder
and cigarettes; a handsome man in a checked shirt
with messy hair and a big grin.
We are the living. We make choices
about who we walk with along white shell beaches.
All of us, even you, will be forgotten,
though possibly not this week.
Blind centuries will rise over our bones, we who once
held hands as we walked down city streets, who
    loved, lost,
ate sweet oranges. The dead feel no jealousy;
they will claim us soon enough. (It is sad, though, that
    the vision
we had of our own great deeds got up and strode into
    the sea.)
Every decision we make in this late afternoon sun
    defines us:
we can wish beauty to stamp us more intensely but
    we move
suffused with the past; when we get up and go, our ghosts,
well-meaning and not, rise with us.
Would you hold out a hand to one?
Only cold ocean-fume will answer
at this turning point of stillness.

The universe speaks in a language like the *Calypso bulbosa*
you've watched send up pink flowers in two days
from the forest floor. A language for holy fools.
The Word resonates from that invisible drum-head
of the world. Have you lit candles for your recent dead?
Some spirits didn't get to say the goodbyes
they would've wanted. So, dance for them.
Lift up your hands, your orchid heart.
They are blooming now in the deep forest.

The surprise of it still stops you: where do they go,
these ghosts? How do they manage without coffee,
the rituals it took a lifetime to collect?
Do even their names get hung up like a coat
you take off inside a door? Certainly
you can feel them, moving like slow meteors
burning with joy. They lean forward as if against
a headwind. They have laid down their worries
about us, fanned them out, cartoon Valentines,
in a shiny heap on a hall table inside the door.
Speculate all you want: the dead may send us
the occasional cheery hello, but their tethers
have snapped, they are all the wild balloon colours
you can imagine and they are disappearing at speed.

Do the dead outgrow us? Perhaps they travel through
such far away passes we no longer catch the flash
of messages they've asked the stars to relay.
Or do the stars forget? They're more into the squeak
and hiss of hydrogen, the electromagnetic colours
of combustion they call music. Left behind,
you bump shoulders with desolation. Again.
If you wait long enough, will the flat world spring back
into breadth, depth, height? Joy has deflated
to a limp word; there is no comfort,
just rolled grey. Only the sun,
your eager dog and daffodils in bloom have meaning.

Each of the dead is sealed, a message in a bottle
spun past us into the roaring cascades of galaxies.
Years ago, after someone you loved died,
that night as you scrabbled between sleep and dream,
unwilling to let go, you struggled with him along
   a steep slope.
No moon, no stars, only a sheen of light
from the sky. At last you reached the rounded arch
of a stone bridge spanning a chasm. A river seethed below;
its cold piercing as a long farewell.
A resonant voice said, *You have followed as far as you
   are able.*
The speaking filled you with awe. You understood then
there were boundaries: you'd pushed too far.
You stopped. Your dead scrambled up to the bridge deck.
Someone was coming: who?
You listened for footsteps as they walked away;
all you heard was the wind hissing, *Water.*

There were seven heavens above Asgard,
city of the Norse gods. Ascending realms of who knows
what festivities, even battle, the Norse might yearn for?
Something profound gutters from a corpse
leaving only a spent candle behind.
Look at the still face you loved. Aren't you surprised
at how *gone* that person is?
You have to ask *where*, and can't they stick around
a bit, help you get your bearings?
Stay at the crossroads at midnight, or on the bridge,
crackling like a transformer with sheer energy.

Here we stand between one
breath and death asking to be light. Off in the distance
the city reflects pink onto the night sky; oh, such
    loneliness
steals the heart and rides off with it hanging
from the saddle. Tell me heaven
is going to be different. Please. We are short-term glories
compared to the integrity of rocks or even trees.
What are we but a rag-bag of longings waiting
to go home? So we ask and receive,
keep believing in that glorious instant
where the universe says, *Yes, it's gold and good,*
until it slips through our fingers like water.

When we vanish from the bodies we've inhabited
and scarred, what quick flame goes where?
Do we hover above ourselves, wonder, *What now*?
Want to comfort our own cooling flesh?
The beauty in us, that thrill of knowing oneself alive,
transmuted now. We become concentrated
to a purity which owns us.
Are there beings in the light that surrounds us?
You squint; it's too intense to see.
Sun reflects from the lake, tiny glitters of bright
like dancing souls. What does it mean to cross over?

If we knew we were dying,
we could plan, yes? Sit together by the fire
with a glass of wine, say, *This is how you will know me.*
But it will always be another year or month, not today
we'll die. Some confide in trees or whisper secrets
into the soft ear of a dog. Light flows through us
until it doesn't, some intangible silver flickers out,
and your beloved falls on a forest path.

The one left behind is violently amazed
at how paper-thin it feels to walk singular
through the world. It is not a good kind of weightlessness.
The empty house rings like a bell with the clapper gone;
waves of panicked air beat against the walls.
Your hands hold nothing. Who are you when you're home?
We define ourselves in relationship: daughter, son,
orphan, lungs, heart, bones, the blue lightning of pain.
The sheltering yew tree, *genius loci* of the garden,
where Anna's hummingbirds perch.
Who are we when even gravity can't define us anymore?
Don't we throw out coils of longing,
soft and thick as braided nylon line, straight up
and ask for messages from our dead? *Give us a sign,*
    a wonder,
we say to the sky. If it obliges, do we believe from hope?
We may be given back a twinkle of spider silk, or six
blue herons who circle us over and over until we weep
for wonder. Or nothing.

Floods of anguish. Then the tide goes out,
which is a good thing, as no organism can sustain
such intensity forever. So you tell yourself
and want to believe.
The closest you get to peace is walking
around the lake. Moving one foot, then another,
hips swing and you're not supposed to call
anyone or do anything other than move.
Juncos keep you company with clicks,
flit from fir to fir. Hold it all like a soap bubble;
be iridescent with love. Keep your hands cupped
softly. We own only our breath.
Love comes with an undated cheque of farewell:
someone has to pay. But cheer up,
it might not be you. Dispute it with the god of doorways.

If only we could stay walking, exist
in that pure moment where we expect only
the pleasure of forward movement,
never have to go home.
Walking, we are as close to transparent as a mountain stream
that in summer, flings itself over rocks in waterfalls
and green pools. We flash yearning toward a cloudless sky.

5

Terror striates our bones. Even if you were too young
to name the dark that sucked your breath,
living bones recorded it in collagen and calcium.
Fear is sharp-clawed. You who were not touched
unless someone hit you, was it surprising
you grew a coiled shell? And still the god of ocean roars
in our veins and we know that sweet tidal surge.
Aren't we all creatures of edges,
of estuaries, where land meets water and falters?
Wind stripes marsh grass as if it were fingers
against fur. It's cold in the transition zone.
Listen to the soft clacking of tall stalks.
Change shows in the genomes
of traumatized organisms to the third generation.
How is this our fault?
Beloved, symmetrical as an ammonite,
your lovely whorls are hard to touch.

We reinvent one another daily. Through sunsets,
through chocolate, through prayer we send out
at night when we wake and know something
is terribly wrong with someone we love. It hurts to be right.
At least, though, we've allowed the invisible real
to move through us and shine.
Tell me goodness leaves a mark in the cold spring air,
that kindness is as immutable as physics, with its own rules
and its own reasons. Tell me fairy tales so we can learn,
all of us, how to behave properly with witches,
to treat animals as our heart-companions.
Let's pull flowing archetypes of nobility over
our ordinary lives: the princess who overcomes,
the hero who sees with the heart.
Clothed in finer narratives, aren't we beautiful?
At best, lovers rescue one another
from worn-soft histories of loneliness, join hands,
say, *Look, we're making ourselves new, together.*

But don't our deepest fears remain constant?
Jörmungandr, the Midgard serpent that girdled the world,
distorts and squeezes our stories. Pressure turns some of us
into shell-creatures, ammonites,
others panic at the scissoring of bleak dark wings
approaching. When one of the lovers dies and one is left,
the survivor must face the snout
of the sea serpent.

Alone.

The dead remain close as our elbows, startling
us with pithy advice about ladders – *You'll find it safer if* –
and simultaneously so absent the air is shocked.
Like the after-sizzle of a flashbulb,
our eyes blink and water. How can we be sure
of two impossibilities at once? Because we also see the third:
our dead laughing, walking toward an unknown
that makes each movement eager.

It's exhausting to hold these bright puzzle
pieces in view, rotate notions like a cool slide
of polished lapis lazuli and moonstones
through our fingers. We own nothing
but the conviction of order. Though it's all a mystery.
And any word from our dead, however infrequent,
is a brief touch from our old warm lives,
the relationship we wore when we loved
who we were.

Anniversaries from the beloved's death
scrape raw gouges into your soft wood,
wear grooves in you.
First you count every day since the death,
then weeks, then, God help you,
months bulk up like continents. Already scars from
    older deaths,
swaths of burn from forest fires,
are greening up. Those loves have gone
beyond now, rocketed off to Antares while
you were buffing your table with beeswax polish
to get some glow back to your life,
make it mean something because that's the fear,
isn't it, all this time on the cloud-swathed earth
that you haven't done what you were meant to, some large
and noble design you've occasionally caught
glimpses of, and lost.
Will your dead be disappointed?
Walk outside to where the firs huddle around
like family. Breathe the clean taste of rain.

How many generations rise up in us when we love,
their memories, their fears coded in our DNA?
We are both singular
as a daisy and immense as the field
it grows in. Our bodies record damage
right down to the cells. Certain music
our ancestors delighted in, circles our shoulders
like a glory of migrating sanderlings. They fan into
    aerial patterns,
collapse,
            then spray into the most beautiful of fractals.
Each of us wants something for the children to come,
who if we are lucky, we will kiss and hold safe
from the cellular whispers
we carry in our blood
and wish we didn't. Making friends with witches
is a tricky business.

We enter into the hall of our grief.
How sharp the air is! And yet, isn't this the task
of being human, to stand in that arched space and open
our arms? Not to step sideways?
We name it and let sorrow's lightning
discharge through us. And it's not like we're free
even then. We move forward companioned with spirits.
This place of desolation is one we will visit
often. It is here we learn to be permeable
as an estuary, to breathe more deeply.
To open our hands.
The winds of life are from the nor'west;
they blow straight through the chest wall to the heart.
These winds shake loose tiny bubbles
of happiness that surprise us:
snow glistens on far blue mountains,
we understand we're kin to the wild yarrow
whose flowers punctuate this green meadow.

The hour of our death is mercifully hidden
in the bottom of a handsome man-purse
of fine Italian leather, what a sheen.
Rummaging through photographs, bank statements,
shopping lists and yellow stickies with love notes,
we can never find what we want until
the gloved doctor adjusts his face mask,
says, *Six months to a year*.
Then we know what we want: for time to wind back
to an infinite line, with ourselves in the middle,
making sweeping gestures like a symphony conductor,
creating exquisite hand-tinted plans.

Three times in the wild, you've glimpsed cougars.
They have the unpredictable beauty
of a waterspout, lethal verbs
that haven't yet struck an unsuspecting noun.
How many have seen a two hundred–foot waterspout
whirl up a glacier-green inlet? The word, *terror,*
isn't harsh enough.

Within three days, everything is loud, jagged.
In hospital, things change so fast
the sharp edges cut into you.

In a hospital a woman feeds yogurt to her love,
a sacrament. Energy surrounds the bed, the hissing
of oxygen, holiness between them pulling
him back to shore.
There's no way she'll let that waterspout have him.
The cougar in the night will come
for us all. But let it be then, not now. Safe.
She wants him safe, and home.
There's a fierceness there you can warm
your hands at. In that room, everything unimportant
has been stripped away, a red jacket a hiker
takes off and lays over a bush, meaning to pick it up
on the way back. And from thousands of miles away,
we say, *Yes, come back. Turn around on the trail.*

We send, as best we can, the silver of willow catkins,
the *kur-aww kur-aww* of a raven high up a fir,
the weight of a dog's head as she leans on a lap.
Who amongst us is ready for transformation?
We want the chance to draw again from the ballots
in Death's purse. Maybe we'll like the next answer better.

Here we stand in a hard place without hope.
What do you mean he won't be coming home?
But he has to, at any moment will walk in the door,
though that anticipated future will never happen.
We apprentice to sorrow. We want the world
to stop, the dozen Canada geese paddling across
the bay to freeze, a halt to the too-sharp
shards of the day that push in at our eyes.

Life is about losing, then gathering
the bright fabric that remains
into pleasing folds: a turquoise hat,
the friend who says, and means it, *You saved
my life*. It is June now: two deaths in four months.
Sun throws magic through maple leaves as you walk.
The green season is dizzy with growth; seals loll on rocks.
Sometimes you feel it's you who turns
while around you, the globe stays still.

Ancestors rise in us.
They surface the way a seal pops into view, swims parallel
as you walk along the shore, light refracting
from its wet head. The ancestors come in dreams.
One says, *Your problems are your salvation*.
The ancestors show up in the turn of a stranger's head
on a crowded street: don't we often see our dead,
or someone so like, we hurry to catch sight of
   a beloved face?

They vanish into a store or turn to speak
with a companion, and we see,
with sorrow chilling as fog,
it's not who we'd hoped. Which we knew anyway,
because their bones are ash, tossed
from the dark spine of a reef at low tide into the sea
while on shore, the rest of us cupped lit candles
as the first sunset visible in weeks reflected
from one orange cloud. Wind from the sea was so cold
our eyes leaked and no seals or birds surfaced,
just the black lick of loss.
Ancestors, speak to us and through us,
we'll take all the wisdom you offer.

What are possessions to the dead?
Less than a puff of air. We, the living,
can arrange them in pleasing patterns; ladders neatly
stowed outside; red glass hummingbird feeder
cleaned and filled; inside, peonies and irises glow
in a Chinese vase on the table. But we hear the ancestors say,
Open your hands. Let life flow through.
Take kindness as a law. Marry it.
What intangible can we leave behind when we go?
A crinkle of affection when someone smiles?
We can't conceive of departure, though we know

the ferryman comes for others.
Why, you, personally, are good for another ten years.
So we move with this bumper of not-seeing death held
    before us,
blankness quivering the air as if it could rub out the
    actual door
we will pass through.
No longer children playing imaginary games,
we work, present ourselves as important or about to be:
see this swift colourful fan of our activity?
The tarot cards of our lives.
We stand in the space between world and toy,
this arm's length consecrated before we were born:
tell us, ancestors, how can we use this time?

We are born carrying our deaths,
the acorn that contains within itself the lightning
which will destroy it.
Our souls know no separation
between ourselves, the soft rooms of air,
the world, the tree. Frame it all gently
between outstretched palms, this innocent time
when the tree *is* us, the acorn is,
the blue-white arabesque of things to come.

You cut through the world, singular now, one
white wake that disperses, sends the tiniest
of ripples onto a pebble beach.
Outside, three pink dogwoods droop under rain,
flowers heavy as hearts.
Trees refuse to believe anything
but the happy snuggle of roots through soil,
chickadees and towhees peeking, triumphant, from
    their canopies.
Oh, we are a circus of broken-world disasters,
the list wearies you: for twenty years
after every dinner with thinking friends, we, like robins,
emerge with beaks full of worm.

      Your man comes home in an urn.

Thoughts float up, pop
like bubbles. Isn't there a tipping point,
where grief becomes so intense it's easier
to allow gravity to smash you flat
than try to rise? You are not strong enough
to save oceans, whales, salmon runs,
or each other.

Who comforts a towhee when it dies?
Your friend once sat with a dying doe
for hours when it collapsed by her back gate.
Witness. I am here, I acknowledge
the pressure of your coming death,
how immense and terrible the dragon-breath
can be. Until, finally, it is not. Stiff
from sitting so long, your friend lurches to her feet,
thinks, *Now I have to bury this deer.*
In the vast clanking scales of giving,
gilded and ornate as clockwork,
many of us are weighed and found wanting.
Some love like heroes.

We stand because this is what our mothers taught us,
because the bowl of sky depends on us to greet it
like a friend. As Luther said,
I can do no other. We belong
on the lawn, gazing up in wonder.
Where do the whispers from our dead
come from? Longing? Break-away angels?
A thread of love?
Sky veers between summer-clear and dubious:
who can we speak to of these months
of enduring? Welcome to the human race.

Loneliness is a fierce tide. Watch it run
in the narrow places of the soul, in raised ridges
of current that hiss as they pass under the one-lane
wooden bridge. This tide will sweep you out to sea
if you're not careful.

Does love leave a shine in the air
if celebrated often enough in the same place?
Walk around the lake, follow the glide
of hundreds of previous walks taken with your love:
you pointed out fresh beaver-work
on the dam to one another, marvelled
at the blue flare of water against sky
as you came down the hill –
is this a real greeting you feel now or longing
reaching through you?
All my mothers, who taught me so much,
none of you told me
loneliness is the great human constant.
Maybe this hard stumble
is a discovery we must make solo,
like stories that twist with the phrase, *And then
I came around a corner and a bear ...*
Days daisy-chain into, *Then what happened?*

We make it up as we go, often hungry,
always amazed to find ourselves propelled
forward by the push of hours: look, spikes
of foxgloves flare now, eccentric sentinels
in the garden, their pink so cheerful, you melt.
You want to keep the garden this green
and luxuriant, long-armed roses humming
into warm pops of brilliance, juncos sheltering
in the canopy of the yew – but the moment breaks free,
an iceberg calving, and the bay swirls
with the currents of long-gone mothers
who smile and say, *We navigated these perilous waters*
between birth and Orion's Belt,
look up, the stars are your friends.
Look up: the stars will guide you safely
home.

Don't we all need something to pattern
from, say, *Self, never mind being human, this yew*
on the hillside that watches over its landscape with arms
outstretched in blessing, copy this instead?
Sacred to the Druids, the yew is death
and resurrection,
the original cross, a tree with branches.
Perhaps we're afraid of the price
of being a hero. It's high risk –
ask Jesus, or Buddha's wife,
abandoned for a bodhi tree.
Wood only ever wants to lean into moving air,
nuzzle up to the turning spray of stars
above its crown.

This morning, wind is a torrent,
pushes evergreen tops in long arcs, rushes between them
noisy with the thrill of its own speed.
Air rustles, full of whirling cedar fronds
and fir branches learning to fly. All these excited ions
wind you up: this is the start of a long storm.
Nine months ago on this green island, your love
went walking in cold January air and then
between one step and the next, died.
You'd like to believe his spirit kept on stepping
right past the end we imagine death to be.
You can't believe life is a line
that finishes with what Aristophanes of Byzantium[*]
called *the terminal dot.*
Period.
Punctuation that stops a sentence.
Finis.

---

[*] In the third century, Aristophanes wanted to show breath. He used three dots, their placement in a sentence determined meaning. Full stop at the end of a complete thought, stigm teleía or "terminal dot"; middle dot, the stigm mésē, a thought resulting in our semi-colon; then hypostigm, or "underdot," which morphed into our comma. From the ninth century on, the full stop began appearing low. Now more than half of all punctuation is the period.

Maybe when we go to the Mystery, we'll see
existence is a wheel or the Norns' tapestry
woven in the wool of ten dimensions;
physicists tell us yes, there are ten.
Your dimension now is cored by absence,
you understand this to your cost.
Days are abalone shells, open to the cloud-filtered sky.
Quite empty.
Such pearl-gleam colours.
It's *Be your own hero* time again. You ask yourself,
what would someone you admire do?
The answer is, *See beauty in the details*.
You are a very mouse of a hero: dun, long-tailed, scurrying.
What can you do but laugh?
It's a bit late to ask for another life.

You yearn to hide from longing but it's a small house.
Longing smells of patchouli and orange candles,
dark musk with a lilt of citrus.
Loneliness buffs the inside of abalone shells, pries open
the book of hours, reads over your shoulder to circle
the full stop you are busy discounting.
Aristophanes, scribes and centuries moved your marks
around on the page, but the meaning's stayed: the end.

But does dying mean a blank page?
Isn't it right there in the hero's
job description: slice through myths, or,
in your case, nibble?
Cretaceous period, Jurassic period,
death is the largest of endings.
Perhaps life simply makes a bend
to another dimension of reality,
the colourful warp of a different story,
a path in the air necessary
when it's our turn to travel the star-road.

Who could imagine we might outgrow desire?
Or at least wrap it in tissue, put it away
with unused treasure? Passion's still there,
we could take it from its high shelf anytime,
or so we console ourselves.
When you lose a love, you mourn as well your own
earlier iteration as one who made celebratory meals,
who crackled with electricity.
Now, in sunshine, with rain pelting in long
  see-through dashes
through bright air, you ask this remaining self,
Who are you at home when no one is watching?
What can you laugh at?
What will you let in through your eyes, the surprise
of this October storm, the hearth fire's orange?
Can you dress to thank the world
for being, for the black and white Dahl porpoises who came
and rode your bow-wave, smiling, in the long-ago?
You are a snapped-trunk arbutus
with berries warmed to the colour of burning coals.

You will never marry again.

Live with it. Smooth it like velvet, purple
under your hands. Dance with it.
The earth is full of others who move into shapes
of attraction, of coming together, their springs
turning toward summers.
Lift up your arbutus hands, bless them with ripe berries,
with wonder that we're here at all in this sough of wind,
our seabirds and whales vanishing like dew –
yet there is still sun and the faith of a dog
who has made you magnetic north,
friends who link themselves with you, gold lines
flung across a continent.

Such fervour pulls the lovers to one another, kisses
on eyelids, the tender skin of wrist, a charge mounting
between them – it makes you tired.
It's a story you've read.
Forgive us, for we know not what we do. We'll do better
tomorrow or next week when we have time to be grateful.
Remember Prague where cobblestones smelled of piss
and you wolfed pear and chocolate pastries
that made you think yes, there is a reason to weep for joy?
Such lightness in a square where tanks rolled in,
    where thousands
of stories collided and changed, wheeling
like birds in the river-scented air.

Now, singular, we learn to wear loneliness, a jewel of sorts,
the colour of a fog bank, sometimes shot through
with blue as moonstones echo sky.
It's a game, isn't it, though poignant,
to replace feeling lonely with merely being alone.
There's the air, the way it touches skin, there are books,
music, the dog, always the dog, snoring or snouting for
    a pat.
Transformation is a silver process, cold much of the time,
slippery, a belt of metal stripping scales you didn't know
you grew on your arms, your legs, your flower heart.
What do we own but air? And then, ultimately,
    not even that.
Inhaling and exhaling, the overlooked gift
of traveling a little longer through this world.
Aren't we all walking one another home?
Home on a turning circle or down the block,
the blaze of a maple turning colour, orange and red
against a dazzle of sky.
How kind shapes are to our eyes,
look at the rusty curl of spent cedar fronds against
    the ground,
the way fractals stamp themselves into our imagination.

Let's not pretend, it's the tender recognition
you sometimes feel in those spaces between the real,
a loon's "O" left on water when it dives,
music that holds out a hand
when you've fallen over a long sad edge,
pulls you back, wet and bedraggled, to shore;
between that struggle and truths
the brain attempts to imagine and slips off,
those out-of-the-corner-of-the-eye loving kindnesses
from the universe you want to hold close;
you connect with a source
that feels like coming home. How strange that we,
who can be so heavy with the hurts of our bodies,
have such aspirations to the ineffable, to want to
    become gold
ourselves, vast and clean.

The unseen world pulls us.
Is turning toward its draw, that huge invisible peace
our goal then, as the certainties
we once counted on, pass away?
To everything there is a season – death,
houses, a carved walnut table made by a
    great-grandmother,
friendships you thought would last a lifetime.
What's left but our dealings with Mystery?
You see, through a prism of bevelled glass, light through
autumn-fire leaves. Colours stroke us on the cheek, sweet
as that sudden clutch of peace the heart feels
sometimes for no reason.

We are the left behind.
Each day trembles with a hole in the air,
a cut-out of the one who walked beside us,
forever, we thought.
Even then, we knew it wasn't true but
couldn't imagine otherwise.
Now here we remain, still standing, though by ourselves:
how extraordinary!
No one who has not borne it can imagine
what a black peony feels like pinned to the heart.
Daily we bear hundreds of repetitions
of the lost one's name. We don't cry out.
Instead we mop floors, devour apples;
the lights are on, the house of our consciousness looks
inhabited and yet –
Bless us, angels, for we are *désolé*. What can we hope
for now?
The black peony is love's highest
token. Congratulations. You too may win it one day.
And yet, isn't there a certain largesse
in such caring? It feels like the extravagance
of feathers on the palm of a hand
or the cool benison of petals. It means,
In this life, we've not been indifferent.
Comfort yourself. The sky has not cut us off, only time.
Don't you love physicists with
their fanned-out deck of dimensions?
Time is only one dimension out of ten.
Nine other dimensions hold a lot of possibilities.

It's hard to stay here. Reinvention hurts like a burn,
continual pain wears at a person,
though this morning you saw a house one green island over
rising from a fog bank, lit in a lozenge of sun.
That helped. As did a flutter of juncos yesterday,
a dozen skittering on the lawn by the cliff garden.
What, exactly, do you hope for?
You'll know it when you feel it,
a tipping of the world back
into beauty, into roundness. Some kind of ease.

What wouldn't we give to move into eternity
as if it were a spring-fed lake where up-welling water
tickles the swimmer?
To swim in light, stroke forward with it,
instead of holding our deaths as the upcoming attraction,
black cut-outs we are inexorably swept toward?
We think we are separate, as if bright threads
could clamber about in their tapestry, as if the *mycorrhiza*
connecting tree roots in the forest you walk daily,
got up and strutted. Really,
our species could mistake
a burning candle for the sun.

We are water. We do the best we can
in this salt season.
All over the world, people die like daisies,
or meteorites; they wither or flame out.
And we mourn.
For those left behind, the absence death leaves
is a vast inaudible clanging.
We are bells who make no sound,
stories paused part-way through.
We feel there's another chapter,
we're not ready to close the book just yet,
we want to know, *And then what happens?*
Ask away, dear one.
Maybe the universe will tell you more
than it has me.
We are the living.
We get to speculate all we want,
wear aqua Liberty scarves with paisley
swirls, eat baked apples fragrant with cinnamon,
to hold our shapes
as best we can in the press of other molecules.
There's a koan if you care to swim it.

Death is a sure animal that moves toward us.
Ask the dead of the pandemic,
the photograph you glanced at this morning,
black-wrapped corpses piled in a hospital corridor
in Russia, thirty deep.
What is it the flame of this world would have us learn?
Combustion? Compassion?
Bless us, for we want our ending
to be one that will make a reader sigh with satisfaction,
pat the book as she puts it down.

Who will you companion with now?
The soft air, full of whirling prayers
butter-yellow as falling maple leaves?
They're not meant to be read by humans.
Perhaps the sedge at the lake's edge
will accept them as currency.
In these short days where darkness
bleeds in from both ends of the hours,
it's best to walk with sun.
Who notices you slip through the days now?
Friends who love you,
perhaps the wind that tousles your hair?

At length, burnished by hard light
from a roaring nor'west wind,
you emerge into spaciousness. Here
at the labyrinth's center, there's no longing.
What a pleasure to stroll through the clean rooms
of your life, held between rocky outcrops bright with moss
thick as your hand.
Green so saturated, it's like being blown a kiss.
You don't dare ask, *How long can this last?*
Tuck worry away like an unbecoming hat.
Stay here with the graciousness of arbutus trees,
cinnamon-coloured inner bark strokable as skin.
Wind has scoured the sky to deep blue, sun
angles in low spears. Winter's coming;
you feel snow in the air's skewer.
Let it pierce you.
Hundreds of feet below, ocean glints
on two sides. Such generosity.
Walk the ridge. Accept this respite from long sorrow,
open your arms to the stillness
              at the spiral's core.

Today, walking in the forest, you could hear ferries sounding
foghorns beyond the island's rim.
Each moment   elongates.
How strangely these cadences impress your heart.
Your dog gambols, an heraldic beast high
on fallen logs, nose outstretched for the treat
that's the payoff for this game.
This fugue of moisture thick in contrapuntal sun
cancels nothing of the hours
you spend awake in the dark, flattened
by how you've failed.
Don't we all have parts in this long-running piece?
You don't want to play anymore.

Here, now, where mist and sun interweave,
small tectonic shocks in the air,
you want to glissando in
between everyone's expectations.
What the world needs now is an intermezzo,
or at the very least
variations on a theme.

For once, your joints feel like silk,
muscles rejoice. Your dog leaps gold
onto the green padded horizontals of a log;
you'd swear she laughs when she takes on a glacial erratic
chest-high on you, scrabbles triumphant onto granite.
The grievous day shifts
                              into stability.

What can the wanderer take across?
We brought nothing into this world
and it's certain we can carry nothing out.
Is praise indelible enough to stay as memory,
the habit you've built so kindly stone by stone,
like the meandering rock wall at home
holding in a foam of pink geraniums?
Surely you'll remember your custom of adoration
for these riches given, a spray of red rose hips,
how one bush lit
the dripping misty forest with amazement?

Argue with the two-faced guardian of thresholds.
You spend your life trying to figure out
the nuances of being here on earth,
the way fear loops
like a noose of wild honeysuckle
about an ankle, then sends you crashing.
A soul has no pockets. Maybe you can smuggle
across a few abstractions like kindness and integrity.

What you've lived by falls away.
Things stay behind.
Old certainties, like rock faces, crumble
into bits of blue shale. You remind yourself
the world has lived through plagues before,
continents have drifted, mammoths
fell to our ancestors. Geologic scale fails
to comfort. You worry about the coming winter, your family,
the child who stands, her back three-quarter turned
from you, long hair flipped over one shoulder.
That girl. That love, immense as an underwater
mountain that shoulders up to become a forested island
with cod nuzzling about its reefs, in one bay,
a giant Pacific octopus snaking one tentacle
over a diver's shoulder to hold him down.
He showed his audience the pictures;
you wished the girl was there with you to go *Ohh*.

Now this winter advances dark as a dive
into deep waters.
Death by Pacific octopus is more common
than you realized.
The tenderness a remembered curve of cheek provokes!
There are many reasons the diver kicks
toward the murky radiance coruscating overhead.

Maybe our deep love of nouns will save us.
A green enamel wood stove
with a copper kettle boiling on it,
the arch of a *clivia*'s strappy leaves,
aren't they minor miracles of order?
How often have you admired the inner bark
of arbutus, its cinnamon strips? Feel how the month
curls about you; confiding, grey, so damp
walking through the woods
is like being fogged with spray from a waterfall.
Once we're gone, what happens to the love
we've felt over and over?
Does it sift into licks of light
from wavetops in a nor'west breeze?

In Plumper Sound, a tideline points
white Vs of foam. The tide's flooding;
from a viewpoint high above the vineyard,
you can see the deep water's uneven pull.

At the end of the day, you want to warm yourself
at the fire of kindness.
Can we take lit candles we've given to others
into the finish of our time?
Around you, neighbours ignite small heroisms
against the coming dark,
orange and warm: one man delivers kindling,
a woman organizes scores of us to make meals
for someone after surgery.
Blessed are those who have friends!
As the world slips toward another lockdown,
we blunder, surprised, into roles
we didn't audition for.

Grief is a season we can't avoid.
You want to emerge shining from this ordeal,
burnished as if you were bronze.
Isn't this our life's meaning,
to learn to love the silver pour
of rain from the roof, lamplit room spacious
with you breathing in what being alone in the world
means? Da Vinci's circle rolls us all in the end.
We waver, naked, toward entropy,
Vitruvian beings, arms and legs akimbo.
What soft answers do we have left?
Only hope and the secrets of sky.

This is a winter of storms with high death tolls,
moments of sun through the toss
of branches. Tree limbs rip, obey gravity,
crash on roofs with fierce abandon.
It's best not to be on the roads.
You mull wind speed
by the volume of roaring. In memory,
the carnival of stories
is in full swing. Many of those who work
at the carnival are runaways. They wear bitterness
like bandannas, insouciant and bright, but there's sadness
to the set of their mouths.
How young they are! This is a better plot point
than the storm, than the narratives they've left behind;
their bravery makes you sigh.
Your chance to win the prize of your choice!
Darts, balls, the wheel of fortune;
everything's rigged, of course, later someone tells you
the *how* of that clacking yellow and black wheel.
Blue pandas the size of a small child, cheapjack toys
and flashing lights, the smell of frying onions,
corn on the cob, the hot-sugar insistence of candy floss.

How can this tawdry energy
barrel forth nostalgic as a steam train?
There's the Bullet, the Ferris wheel, the roller coaster,
screams from people who pay
to be terrified.
How did you get here? When can you go?
Of all the rides, the vintage merry-go-round
is the one that draws you; painted wooden horses
with manes and tails like charms
stream in the calliope wind. You prefer fairy tales
with safe endings.

Today, a whirl of pine siskins erupted
from the leafless tree outside your kitchen window,
tiny, streaky-brown, all coordinated.
Here then *gone*. A flock,
too many to count.
Half an hour later, you still replay
their precision. Maybe some farewells need
to be said over and over, another stone added
to the cairn that marks where your love died.
An ephemeral art project, the Parks people
agreed to call it.

You hope something like the storm of perfect birds
ushered him across the air he stepped away from then,
something benign, lovely as a spray of holly
berries or an opening of blue sky
after long rain.
Each time you nestle a rock on the cairn,
you say *Hello* and *Goodbye*.
It's hard to know which hurts most.
You don't want to walk forever
with laments. Too much like being rubbed out
by sea-fog.

You'd prefer to cherish the small particulars
that life offers, kingfisher colours
fanned out, an astonishment
of hand-painted silks on a craft-fair table:
you know perfectly well by the end of the day,
all those marvels will be packed up or sold,
even the tables will be disappeared to some
far cupboard, leaving a bare room full of echoes.

Ten months your love has been gone from hugs,
into a fringed blue elsewhere you can't imagine.
But the persistence of objects!
Today you staggered with a rock almost too heavy
to prise up, to his cairn, moss on your burden
green as a question.
Did the world used to astonish you so much?
It does now, whorls of objects
washed up like abalone fragments on a beach,
at dusk, the dark shapes of evergreens
stamped ecstatic against a lighter sky.

Alone, you are closer to the infinite, or at least
not dodging its background hum, with starfields,
the soft squorbbling of harlequin and bufflehead ducks,
the extraordinary conviction
that envelopes you sometimes, of love,
how the language of mountains,
the cheer of chicory flowers that snatch your heart
with their ragged boutonnieres of sky,
are runes you can't yet decipher, but will some day.

ACKNOWLEDGMENTS

Special thanks to Adelia MacWilliam who gave me feedback on the first iteration of the poems. We've been workshopping buddies for decades: what a blessing!

I'm grateful to Kate Braid and Sandy Shreve who read more polished versions and offered wonderful suggestions.

I appreciate the fierce care, love, and enthusiasm from all of you!